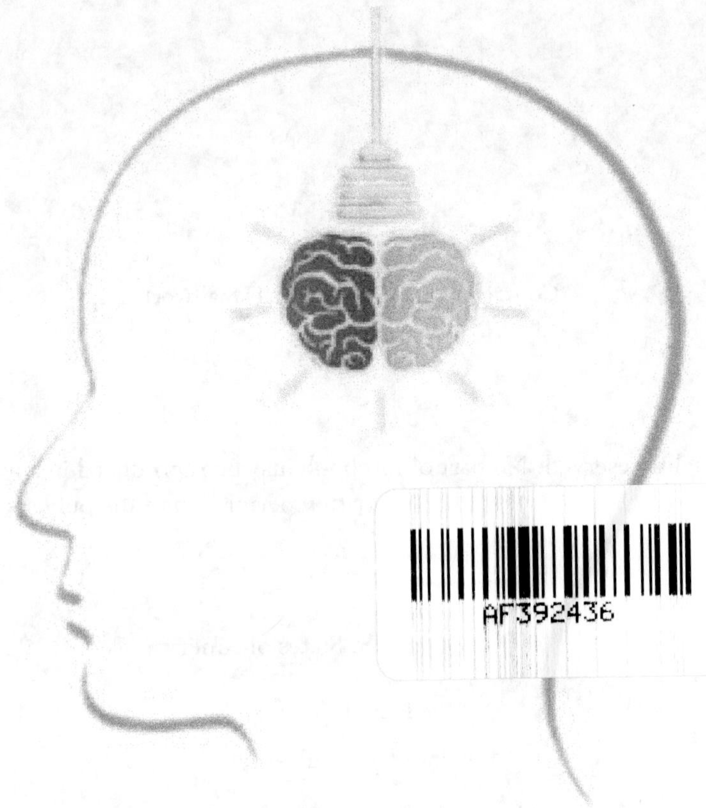

LOST AND FOUND

LEWIS D. STALLWORTH III

Printed in United States of America

Published By

HemingWay Publishers 2023

www.hemingwaypublishers.com

TABLE OF CONTENTS

LOST AND FOUND
Mark 4:35-41

INTRODUCTION

Today, many people are not sure of what their purpose in life is. We believe that our purposes are to be doctors, lawyers, mothers, husbands, handsome men, and beautiful women. The goals of many young men are to be the Mac daddy of all Mac daddies, and many young women have set out to be the hoochie mama of all hoochie mamas. We truly believe that these are the purposes that God placed us on this earth for. In studying this text, I was enlightened on the fact that a person who gives up his or her life and loses it in the body of Christ will find himself or herself.

> **Matthew 1-:39** reads, "He that findeth his life shall lose it: and he that loseth his life for my sake shall find it."

> **Matthew 16:25** reads, "For whosoever will save his life shall lose it: and whosoever will lose his life for my sake shall find it."

Have you ever lost something precious, and you couldn't remove the thought that you had lost it out of your mind? There are certain things that I have lost, and I want them back with all of my heart.

I can recall the first ring that I purchased for my wife. I spent hard-earned money to buy that ring. One day, we were at my mother's house, and she took the ring off to wash her hair, and when she finished washing her hair, we couldn't find it. At that time, the ring that I purchased for her was the best that I could afford. It didn't cost a lot of money, but I spent all that I had on it. The ring meant a lot to me because I gave it to her with all my heart. It was a symbol of how I felt about her, and every dollar that I spent on it meant something. By giving her that ring, I was letting her know that I loved her and I wanted her to be the woman that I would marry.

This is how God feels when it comes to you and me.

We are too comfortable down here. I want you to know that you have lost your beginning. I also want you to know that you can change your ending. Right now, your ending says that this world is going to become rougher and rougher, people are going to steal from you and lie to you, that sickness, malice, and strife will be upon you, and you will always have to work, have shots, and take medicine. We were never created for all of these lies, hatred, high blood pressure, and heart problems. We were created for the glory of God to be in our presence and to talk to and have a relationship with Him in a peaceful environment.

It's time to find that which was lost. I've lost something, and I can not become comfortable living here. I am tired of having an upset stomach, having to take a vacation because I have too much stress, and having my medicine cabinets full of Tylenol, codeine, and Vicks. I wasn't made for this. I was made to be in peace, and I have to find it.

The devil is trying to rob us. Right now, the devil wants us to focus on our past; however, we can't change the past. The prodigal son could not change the fact that he wasted all of his money. All that he could do was return home with what he had. Some of us need to return to God with what we have. And what we have in our possession is more than what the devil has. The devil doesn't have anything. We at least have a chance. The devil doesn't even have that much. All we have to do is tell God that we are sorry. The devil doesn't want us to do that. He doesn't want us to ask God to forgive us and save us. Satan knows that once God forgives us, everything begins again from the beginning.

Some of us are in a situation where God is trying to use us, and we are standing in His way. God has called us to preach, and we want to work in music. Every time the anointing comes upon us, we run from it. We quench the spirit and begin to think. God wants you to know that He didn't tell us to think; He told us to receive Him. Do not delay the revelation of your life's purpose by trying to find it on your own. Turn yourself in to the lost and found today. There is business in the kingdom of God that has been set aside for you to do.

FINDING THE LOST

What we must first understand is that we are in possession of God. God has created us and made us in the image of His likeness. God loves us so much that when we follow the devil, he loses his mind. He can't take losing us to Satan because he is a jealous God. Anytime that we give the devil God's glory, it upsets him. At the same time, he has a different reaction when we acknowledge that we did, in fact have turned away from God and that we have now decided to turn back to Him. When God sees that we've done those things, everything that we've lost, He'll return to us. This is one of the things about God that the devil doesn't want us to know. Anything that God gives us has our name on it, and it belongs to us. No one else is made to have the things that God has given to each of us. Anything that God has for us is only for us.

Have you ever been around a mother who has lost her child? When someone comes into a mother's house and takes her child away, she can't sleep; she paces the floor, puts up posters, stays on the phone, and goes back and forth to the police station. She does all of this because she's lost something that meant something to her. This is how God is. God wants you to know that He has lost a soul that meant something to Him.

This is why every time one soul is returned to God, and every time He gains His possession back, He throws a party in heaven. He tells the angels that what was lost, He has found, and it's back in His possession. The thing that He missed is that He now has it back, and He wants to celebrate.

There isn't anything in this world that compares to having something that is valuable and precious to you and one day finding out that it is roaming around out of your protection and someone else has their hands on it. There isn't anything that is similar to investing in something, putting your time into it, and suddenly finding out that it's become someone else's possession.

I can recall a time when my mother and I went to Texas. When we arrived there, my mother gave me a leather jacket that belonged to her brother. I remember wearing that jacket at school, and I knew that someone else had my jacket. There wasn't anything worse than walking around school and asking everyone who had my jacket and where it was. Every time I saw someone wearing a jacket that was similar to the color of the jacket that my mother had given me, I wanted to walk up to them and see if the jacket had my name on it.

The reason why Jesus is the way that He is today is that He has lost something. He has lost people who were created to praise Him and lift Him up. These days' people give more praise to books, the internet, politics, the government, and everything else in the world than they give to God. Jesus Christ is saying that He's lost something, and He can not rest until He has it back in His possession.

God is similar to the woman that lost a coin (**Luke 15:8-10**). Her one coin may not be of any value to anyone, but when you don't have money, and you know that right now you have a coin that is worth something, and when you look for it, it's not there, and your bills are due, and your car is out of gas, that one coin is worth a lot to you. You search all over for that lost coin because you know that it has value. This is how Jesus is today. He knows that we are of value. He knows how important we are in the body of Christ.

I'm unaware of what your problems are. I don't know what has led you away from God. What I do know is that you need to check yourself into the lost and found. You need to say, *"Here am I. Turn me back into the Master, to the Christ, to the I AM THAT I AM, to Jehovah Jirah."*

This is the reason why we have to be turned in to the lost and found. We have to go back to the place where Jesus covered us and surrounded us, the place where the anointing and the power are. I don't know about you, but I'm beginning to grow weary of roaming around this world being lost and mixed up. I'm tired of not knowing who I am. I'm tired of changing occupations, schools, and clothing to try to fit in, and when I've done everything to try to change, I realize that I still don't fit in.

Today, I'm glad that I've turned myself into the lost and found and to the Creator, who knows the number of hairs that are on my head and knows when every sparrow falls out of the sky. I'm unaware of your situation, but I grew tired of being someone else's possession. Someone who didn't truly know me. Someone who didn't honestly care about me. Someone who didn't think anything of me, someone who wanted to steal from me and kill and destroy me. Someone who was jealous of me. Someone who misused and abused me.

This is how Satan treated me. He didn't treat me the way that the woman who lost her coin treated her coin. He didn't put me inside a package so that dust and rust wouldn't corrupt me. Maybe Satan has been good to you, but that isn't my testimony. Satan used me up, dogged me out, and sent me to travel from one coast to another coast. Now, I'm glad that Jesus went to the cross for me, that I was on His mind when He took those nails for me. I'm glad that He took those licks for me and that He suffered and died for me so that I may be found. Now, I'm living in a time period of grace.

God said that we don't have to worry any longer. If we find that we are lost, it's best for us to stand where we're at and ask the Lord to forgive us for our sins. He said that His grace will be with us, and this is why I'm glad. I was similar to the prodigal son who returned home.

Today, some of us need to come to our senses. The devil is using and mistreating us. We are out in the hog pen. We smell bad, and we're dirty. God wants us to know that we don't have to live that way. We need to realize that a man who loses his life shall find his life.

Ever since the day that I walked down to the altar and asked the Lord to forgive me for my sins and confessed that I betrayed Him, my attitude and my mind have been different. Now, I have a purpose and a destiny in my life. I have a future and hope in my life. I'm glad that He saved me and raised me. There isn't anything worse than being in someone's possession when that person doesn't care about you. Jesus wants us to know that He feels what we feel. He's been through the same things that we are going through. He carried His load for 33 years. He knows what it is to go through something, to be arrested, to feel pride, and to feel hungry. We need to turn ourselves back into the lost and found.

We do not belong to the devil; we belong to God, and every hair that is on our head belongs to Him. With that in mind, I must ask why many of us are serving the devil and listening to him. Why are we giving him praise, glory, and honor? You may say, Elder Stallworth, I'm not doing all of those things.

Revelation 3:15-16 reads, "So then, because thou art Luke warm, and neither cold nor hot, I will spume (spit) thee out or my mouth."

Matthew 6:24 reads, "No man can serve two masters: for either he will hate the one, and love the other; or else he will hold to the one, and despise the other. Ye cannot serve God and mammon (money)."

We have to give God all of the praise and all of the glory. God doesn't want half of the praises that He is supposed to receive. God is not comparable to these 90's women who want half of a man's money. God desires our all. It is time that we turn ourselves into the lost and found and tell the Lord that we are presenting ourselves to Him and that we are the ones who are standing in need of prayer. We need to tell God that He can use our hands, feet, mouths, hearts, tongues, and minds.

I've decided that I am going back to get what belongs to me. I don't need all of the crazy things that this world has to offer. If I lose both of my legs trying to obtain what belongs to me, then so be it. I'll give up my flesh to receive what God has for me. Regardless of what I leave without, let me have what is mine.

God has prepared a place for us that has not been made by hand, and the streets are paved with gold. Where there are pearly gates and angels are singing. There, we don't have to worry about sickness and diseases. This place is ours, and all that we have to do is seek God to abide there. God said that if any man hears His voice, He will not harden our hearts.

One of the things that I love about God is that He chose me when I was lost and thought that I was unable to be found in a world of sin. There is something special about when God finds you. I've heard people say that they found God. However, the truth is that God found them.

God is married to the backslider. I've been reading about what Jesus says about a married man. He should love His wife as Christ loves the church and be willing to give his life for his wife. God wants you more than you are aware of. Throughout the Bible, God explains ways to influence you to return to Him. There are things such as the parable of the lost sheep. God says that he loves us so much that He's not going to wait for us to come back to the foe; He's going to come and find us Himself.

Has God ever come and rescued you right where you were at? You were caught in the act of sin, and He came and found you. He didn't wait for you to find your way back home. Some of you don't want to come back home. The same is true of a shepherd who goes to find a sheep that has strayed away. When he finds the sheep and it doesn't want to come home, the Shepherd will break its leg, put it on his shoulder, and walk home.

Has God ever talked to you? At the sound of His voice, He begins to speak life into you, and He restores your soul. It's fine when your mother tells you that everything is O. K., but there's something different when God tells you that everything is going to be O. K.

You have to realize how much you mean to God. You can leave Him if you'd like to because He'll find you and bring you back.

Psalms 23:6 reads, "Surely goodness and mercy shall follow me all the days of my life: and I dwell in the house of the Lord for ever."

FOR PASTORS AND LEADERS

From the very first time that the doctor slapped us on our backsides and we inhaled the air of the earth into our bodies, God had already known specifically what we were going to be. There is a specific reason why God allowed us to be birthed into this world. The purpose that God has for our life has not been predestined for our personal use. Our purpose has been given to us so that God can be glorified. Right now, some of us are fighting within ourselves because we don't want to be that man or woman of God, which is what God purposed us to be. We have yet to realize that this purpose that God has given us is the very thing that we were created to do.

We have begun to spend too much time trying to search for ourselves in colleges, in our communities, and through our friends. The problem is that while we are doing those things, we never find ourselves. Actually, we become even more of a lost person by trying to find out who we actually are on our own and according to our own tactics. Eventually, we look around and see that we are roaming around, unaware of what we are supposed to be doing because we have yet to figure out what we were created to do.

Every man and woman who enters into this world has already been given a general purpose. That general purpose is to give God praise, to give God glory, to worship Him, and to have a relationship with Him. The more specific purpose is exactly how we are to do those things, which is known as our calling. Most of us are more into what we believe our purpose is than what God has said our purpose is. We are more into things like our occupation, ourselves, and our education.

The more that I have been unleashing and releasing the worldly things that I had grown to be attached to, the more I have begun to come to Christ and say, Lord, here am I. I am beginning to find myself. I'm finding out what I am really made of and why I was made this way. I'm finding out why my mind thinks the way that it does. I'm finding out why my attitude is the way that it is.

I'm finding out all of these things because I have lost myself at the foot of the cross. I've given up everything that I have. God wants us to know that if we are going to be with Him, then we must take up our crosses and follow Him.

> **Matthew 10:38** reads, "And he that taketh not his cross, and followeth after me, is not worthy of me."

To discern this statement spiritually, you must understand it naturally. A cross is something heavy. It's a burden. Carrying a cross for an extended period of time eventually becomes a tedious act. Therefore, what God is saying is that we need to go through some of the things that He has gone through. The problem that we have is that we don't want to carry our crosses. We don't want to suffer. We don't want to go through any of the things that God has gone through.

I am also finding that there is a way for us to find our purpose. That way is not by searching on our own. It's not by searching through and in men and women. What we need to do is turn ourselves into the lost and found.

Some of us may be in a situation where God has been trying to obtain our attention, but worldly things caught our eye. God wants us to know that He needs us to take care of kingdom business. There is no greater time than this to go into business with God. He is not going to let the devil receive more praise and glory than Him. Right now, there are men who have sold out to everything the devil has offered them. When you mention their jobs, they immediately run to them. If their boss calls, they run to do what he asks. Sometimes, their boss doesn't have to call. You can go to their jobs on a Sunday and find them at their desk. Yet, the church is lacking, and the body of Christ is hurting because the men and women that God created to make His church complete are in the world working for the devil.

He told the people that if there is anything about Him that they should know, it would be the fact that since He was a child, He had practiced being dogmatic to the men and women of the church *(Acts 26)*. He said that anything that he was involved in, he was wholeheartedly involved in it. Paul gave up those activities on the road to Damascus when Jesus spoke from heaven and said, "Saul, Saul, why persecute thou me? **(Acts 9: 3-9)**"

Men and women need to begin to step into the anointing. We need to become sellouts.

> **Matthew 6:25** reads, "Behold the fowls of the air: for they sow not, neither do they reap, nor gather into barns; yet your heavenly Father feedeth them. Are ye not much better than they?"

If He makes way for dogs in the street to eat and survive, aren't we much greater than a door? If the Lord provides mild food for cats, aren't we much greater than a cat? So many men and women are afraid to try God. I don't have anything else to lose. That's exactly why I'm going to become more vile and more radical than I am now. I have given up everything that I had, and I've come to find that this walk with God is becoming sweeter and sweeter.

Every time we go against what God has said, or we go against the word of God, we go directly against God. We're not hurting ourselves as much as we are hurting God. We're hurting God because the business of His kingdom suffers when we are not fulfilling the purpose that He has for our lives. God wants to use us. There are some of us who have been told by God to pray for someone, and we say that we couldn't do it. By not doing what God said to do and going against His word, we've hurt the kingdom's business. To some of us, God has said that he wants us to give up our very lives, our souls, our hearts, our thoughts, and all of our time to the body of Christ. We responded by saying that we couldn't do that because we had bills to pay. By doing that, we exalted our bills above God.

I don't know what has led you away from God, but it's time for you to lose yourself in God. The things that are going on in the body of Christ today are things that I have never seen before. So many ministers are more wrapped up in their own personal problems than they are in handling the business of the kingdom of God. Out of the 39 books and 929 chapters in the New Testament, I have yet to read a verse where the disciples were worried about their problems. It was always kingdom business with the disciples. Paul was so serious about God and taking care of his business with the kingdom of God that he wished that all of us would be like him and wouldn't get married **(1 Corinthians 7:7)**. That is how serious things were in Paul's time. This was a time when a man would give up his sex life in the prime of his youth to follow God and take care of kingdom business. Paul preached in front of kings and the most regarded men at that time, and he never went into his personal affairs. Regardless of his own situation, Paul always lifted up the name of Jesus.

This is what God wants from us. God wants people who are willing to sell out to handle His business. Paul was a sellout. We've sold out to the devil. Some of us have done things that were so evil or sinful that if our parents knew about it, they may want to disown us. If the body of Christ knew some of the things that we did in private and in the dark, they wouldn't even want to talk to us anymore. We've said that we would never do this and we would never do that, and the first thing that we did when we gave in to Satan was exactly what we said we wouldn't do. Right now, in the body of Christ, people are worried about their personal cares, and none of them are worried about carrying out kingdom business.

God once said to me, "Why is the world seeking and going crazy? Why do they have the best out there [in the world], and my church is lacking? Where are all [of] the sellouts? I won't have anything above me. I'm a jealous God. Why aren't the people seeking me instead of seeking the world? They give their all in the world. They change their clothes and their attitude, cut [their] friends off. Why don't they do that for me? Am I not worthy? They sell out with contracts for years, and some of them know they're going to be dogged and mistreated. Some of them know they're going to have to sleep with the top man, but they do it to get there. Why don't people do that for me? If you can hear what I'm saying, the sky is the limit."

SATAN'S WORK

We have to understand that the devil begins to talk to us once we are entangled in a state of sin. He begins to tell us that we will not rise from our sin and we will not be able to escape it. Furthermore, we must realize that whatever has been lost can be found. Understand that when we come to God, He will forgive us and return to us those things that we have lost.

I once told a man, "When I was a young man, I messed up a lot. I had a lot of errors. Now, God is punishing me for the things that I did when I was young."

The man responded, "Wait a minute, young man. You don't believe that we are serving a God who, if you were to tell that you were sorry and asked Him to forgive you for your sins, would punish you eighteen years later? You don't really believe that, do you?"

"Yeah, I do."

"No. Look at this. You are a preacher, and you are saying that God will punish you after you have asked Him to forgive you. God is not that type of a god. God is not that small that He would keep thinking about petty things after you have repented and begun your first works over again."

This is exactly what the devil doesn't want us to understand and recognize. The truth of this matter is that although we can not change the past, we can change the direction of the future. Satan wants us to dwell on the past. We can not change the things that we did yesterday, but we can change what we are going to do tomorrow. We can make our minds up to do good or to do bad. There is no way for us to go back and relive yesterday, a week ago, or two years ago.

The reason why most of us have so many problems is that we dwell on the past too much instead of looking into the future. We don't realize that our past is over; it's history. But what we have the power to work on today is our future. Yesterday, we may have been liars, but today, we can be the men and women that God has called us to be. We have to understand that the devil wants to keep us focused on our past so that our past begins to haunt us. When the devil talks to us, he always brings up our past. He brings up things such as the fact that we didn't pray earlier today, we didn't read our bible, and the way we had an attitude that day. I want you to know that if you can remember that God is forgiving, you can say that you're sorry about the things that you didn't do, but what you are going to do is start living right from this moment forward.

Some of us need to come to our senses and realize that if we go the wrong way, there has to be a right way for us to come back. Know that there is a reason why our hearts are still beating, and God hasn't taken us out of this world. If God didn't destroy us for our sins, we should know that there has to be a reason why we are still living. If God was, in fact, as mad as the devil has said that He was, then our hearts would have stopped beating, and our blood would have begun to run cold in our bodies. Understand that if we are still here, God still loves us. We have to keep in mind that the devil is a liar. We must be aware that God waits for our aching and painful return. He waits for us to do an about-face and turn back to Him. The devil tells us that we've gone too far, we've said too much, and we've been sitting down too long. None of that is true. Like the father of the prodigal son, God is waiting, anticipating, and looking for us to return to Him and begin our first works again. He's waiting for us to talk to Him again. He's anticipating us opening up our Bibles and beginning to read His world again. The situation was the same with the prodigal son. When he began to walk away, his father said that he knew that his son would return, so he'd continue to look for him.

We have to understand that the devil was created to bring havoc into our lives, to make our lives miserable, and to torment us. Satan wants to make our lives so bad that we feel as if the only way that we can find peace is to return to our original Father. Sometimes, we take on a role that is different than what God planned for us. I want you to know that if you return to your original Father, your original God, He will wipe away every tear, hardship, and pain that you have. The devil doesn't want us to go to God. The Lord wants us to know that in every test, we're going to grow stronger and stronger. The devil doesn't want us to realize that we are made of flesh and that flesh makes mistakes. This is why God says, "My grace is sufficient."

The devil tells us that we are not going to change, that we are not going to be able to shake off our sins, that our sins have been in our family's bloodline, and that we don't have a choice whether or not we are going to act a certain way. He tells us that we've been telling the same lie for years and that we've been acting the same way for our entire lives, so there is no way that we are going to change. He tells us that our sins are always going to be with us. I want you to know something: the Bible says that because of one man's sin, we were separated from God in the Garden of Eden, and all of us fell short of the glory of God **(Romans 5:12).** Since we became separated from God, he has been waiting for our return. He said that there would be a day when He wouldn't give up on His people. He said that He would wait and anticipate them coming back and wait until their change came for them. God wants you to know that He has nothing but time, and since we were His in the beginning, we will be His in the end, and He is going to wait for our return.

KEEP LOOKING

Sometimes, we have to keep pressing our way through until we receive our breakthrough, our victory, and our joy. Often times, we have to keep standing in the prayer line until we find that which is lost. Sometimes, when we lose something in our house, we have to keep backtracking again and again until we find it.

When I was a child, my mother would use me to find keys that were lost in the house because I wouldn't stop looking until I found them. I would look in cracks, clothing, and everywhere else I could think of. The other kids would give up. I knew that I couldn't quit or give up because there was a reward for me if I found the keys. My mother told us that whoever found the keys would receive five dollars, and I needed that five dollars. So, I wouldn't stop looking for the keys because I didn't have what I needed.

Some of us don't have the things that we need, but we've ceased looking.

Paul says in **(Philippians 3:14)**, "I press toward the mark for the prize of the high calling of God in Christ Jesus."

Why do you suppose that Paul said "press"? He said it because it's not going to be easy; it's going to be hard. Sometimes, we'll have to crawl, cry, and step over people to seize our breakthrough, but we have to press on anyhow. We have to tell our flesh that we're going to find those things which are lost. The devil doesn't want us to accept in our minds that we have lost something.

I have been reading in the Bible about Paul and Peter, the two brothers who are spoken of in the gospels **(Matthew 4).** These two men gave up everything that they had to follow God and become disciples of Jesus Christ. Today, I don't see that happening in the body of Christ. I still see preachers who are holding on to certain things. I still see singers who are holding on to certain things. Paul decided to let go of everything that he had. His possessions didn't mean anything in comparison to what he found he could have with God.

What are we holding on to today? What is in the world that has distracted us from focusing on God? Was it what we heard on 92.3 The Beat while we were on our way to church? Was it that beautiful girl who had long hair and green eyes? Was it the money that we've grown to love so much? What was it that caught our attention and led us out of the Master's hand? If the Master can control the sea, why do we believe that He's incapable of controlling our lives? My Bible tells me in **Mark (4:35-41)** that the disciples were on a ship, and the ship was being tossed with waves. Jesus stepped onto the water and said, "Peace be still **(verse 39)",** and the sea became calm.

I was talking to a young lady once who didn't believe that Jesus could calm the sea that was raging around her. If Jesus can calm a sea that had qualified fishermen in it, men who knew how to deal with harsh waves, men who knew how to make the ship go left and right, why is it that we believe that He can't calm our seas? The men on this boat were afraid when Jesus said, "Peace be still." the waves ceased from tossing the ship. These men, in astonishment, said that even the waves and the seas obey Christ. Understand that this woman I spoke to had been caught up in the cares of the world, and she didn't believe that Jesus could calm her sea. She was caught up in her money and believed that she had to have everything.

If I had to serve a God who couldn't take care of me, then I would stop serving him. If I found myself serving a God who was weak and jelly-backed, I would have to let him go. Those characteristics do not describe the God that I serve. The God that I serve has all power, and it has been given unto Him in heaven and on earth. God said that whatever I ask for in His name, it shall be done. Anything that God speaks into existence from His tongue will come to pass so that His Father, who is in heaven, will be glorified.

Most department stores have a lost and found department. Many times, people go into a store and leave their wallets. They go back to the store the next day and ask one of the store employees where the lost and found department is located. They explain that they were in the store the previous day and that they had left their wallet. They tell them that when they backtracked over the activities that they did the day before, they realized that the last place that they used their wallet was in this store and that they needed their wallet back. They need their possessions.

Today, we, as the body of Christ, need to begin to backtrack and find some of the things we have lost. You will come to find that in the spiritual realm, the things that we have lost, God is waiting for us to come back and find. We often believe that we can not return to God and receive our lost possessions because we were like the prodigal son, and we, too, have lived a riotous lifestyle. The things that God has given to us are precious. We have taken them and went into the world and used them to live our riotous lifestyle. Some of us have taken our anointing, our talents, our bodies, and our joy into the world.

AMBASSADORS OF CHRIST

2 Corinthians 6:17-21

INTRODUCTION

I am the pastor of Christ Temple Church of Los Angeles, California. In church, my members, as well as myself, realize that it has been the way that we praise and worship God that has brought us to the place that we are today. When we first began, we were on Slauson Street in Los Angeles, and there were windows in the church where people would pass by and see us jumping around the church and acting crazy. I always kept in mind what **Matthew 10:32-33** reads,

> "Whosoever therefore shall confess me before men, him will I confess also before my Father which is in heaven. But whosoever shall deny me before men, him will I also deny before my Father which is in heaven."

Due to the fact that we weren't ashamed of Jesus before man, He was not ashamed of us before His Father. Jesus couldn't withhold any good things from us because we weren't ashamed of Him. However, people said that we weren't ashamed of Him.

Although people said that we weren't saved and sanctified, we continued to praise Him. Every time we praised Him, He had to leave His throne in heaven and hover over us because He inhabits the praises of His people **(Psalms 22:3)**.

John 12:32 reads, "And I, if I be lifted up from the earth, will draw all men unto me."

When God is lifted above our problems, circumstances, feelings, pride, and situations, He comes through for us in an amazing way. This is the reason today my church is able to give God praise in a new sanctuary, at a new appointed time, at a new hour, and during a new year.

You are an ambassador of Christ. The only reason why you are living at this present moment is for Christ. The only reason why you have eyesight is because of Christ. The only reason why you have the ability to hear is because of Christ. Our lives don't have anything to do with us.

DEFINING WHO YOU ARE

You have no excuse not to be another Paul or another Peter. God has chosen some of you, and you knew that you shouldn't have been the one that God chose. Some people have been in church for fifteen and twenty years, and you've only been with God for six or seven months, and they are nowhere near where you are in God, and God is using you profoundly and awesomely.

You've heard enough of the word to be able to save yourself, but the word hasn't penetrated you because you don't know who you are. The truth is that you are someone, and the devil is trying to trick you even as you read this book. What God is about to do will literally blow your mind. This is why the devil is trying to throw us off with a lot of crazy things.

There are three ways that you can sin (1 John 2:16):

1. The lust of the eyes.

2. The lust of the flesh.

3. The pride of life.

The devil is getting to many of us with pride. We don't have two dollars in our wallet, yet we don't want anyone to tell us anything concerning our finances. People need to realize that they can not afford to behave that way. When people come to you and tell you something, recognize that they are coming to you in love. Love will look beyond your faults and see your needs.

BREAKING TRADITIONS

The only reason we are here in this particular place, at this appointed time, is Jesus. I noticed that many people were not supportive of my church. Many people were not coming around and saying that they wanted to partake in this great thing that was happening in my church. I soon came to realize that the reason why people were not drawing towards my church was because they were stuck in tradition. Right now, God is allowing people to step out of tradition and draw towards Him. He is doing this because you are an ambassador of Christ. You do not come in your own mind, your own thoughts, or your own ways. You come representing the number one man, spirit, name, and force.

Do not allow others to trick you. You are an ambassador of Christ. You have to give an account to God for every deed that you carry out. Do not allow people to hold you back because of their traditions **(Matthew 15:3-9)**. God is not coming back for the church of God in Christ, the Apostolic, the Baptist, or the Methodist. God is returning for people who have made themselves ready—a person who is without a spot or wrinkle or anything similar. We have too many divisions and drawbacks in the body of Christ. We need everyone to put on their armor and fight.

It is a shame for a Muslim not to have the Holy Ghost. Suppose he'll still take a stand with a bean pie or a newspaper. Imagine what he could do with God. There are some Muslims that I have talked about and spoken out of line to, yet they still stood fast with their bean pies and their **"Asalaam-u-akliam"** greeting, and they wouldn't allow anyone to change them. Where are the men and women of God who are willing to stand fast and proclaim that they are not about to allow anyone to change them?

> **1Peter 2:9** reads, "But ye are a chosen generation, a royal priesthood, a holy nation, a peculiar people; that ye should shew forth the praises of him who hath called you out of darkness into his marvelous light."

To show forth means to come out of or bring out of hiding. Bear in mind that you have been delivered and set free. Do not return to bondage. Separate yourself and come from among the unbelievers.

God took a cold-hearted man by the name of Peter and allowed him to begin a revolution for Jesus. When the men came to arrest Jesus, Peter still had his sword. He tried to kill one of the soldiers with it, but he cut the man's ear off. Jesus told Peter to put his sword away. He told Peter that if he lived by the sword, he would die by the sword. It is amazing to me that Peter carried a sword while he walked with Jesus, yet Jesus told him that He would give him the keys to the kingdom of heaven **(Matthew 16:19)**. Why didn't God give the keys to a priest or to those men and women who were making sacrifices at that very moment? It was because they were stuck in tradition.

I'm only making you aware of these things so that you will come out of your traditions and do God's will. There is great work for you to do. If you try to appear to be holy and dignified, you'll never save the world. That isn't what the world wants. The world wants someone who will penetrate the places where they are hurting. They want someone to reach their pain and save them.

As a young boy, I would see preachers stand in front of the pulpit with their arms stretched out as if they were high and mighty men. People would walk up to them, hurting and with tears in their eyes, and the preacher would begin a traditional spiritual prayer. When they were finished, those people would go back to where they were in an even worse condition because they went before the preacher believing that God was able to move for them, and people played games with them.

I don't want anyone to play games with me. This is the life that we are dealing with. I only have one life and one soul. I don't want anyone to play church with me. I arrive at church needing something that is going to penetrate down to the inside of this man. I don't want people to look at my outer man; I want someone to look inside of me, as Jesus looks beyond our faults and sees our needs.

This is why we have to begin to have church the correct way. Wherever Jesus went, He had a church service. He made sure that everyone was there. Read it for yourself. He defeated every type of disease and sickness. We shall do a greater work. Jesus had people who would attempt to hold Him back, hinder Him, and try to kill Him. There is no one trying to kill you. You can go all across the world. There is no excuse; the word of God is in almost every country. During earlier times, when men went wherever they wanted to go, they died. Peter wasn't able to do everything that he wanted to do. They were going to crucify him, but he said that he wasn't worthy of being crucified like Jesus. So, they hung him upside-down and killed him.

On the other hand, there's no one thinking about if you're not doing anything productive for God. You're not even on anyone's mind. No one is knocking on your door telling you to stop preaching and laying hands on people because you're not doing it. You have a clear path to do whatever you want.

TIME TO CHANGE

You have to understand that you are representing a name that does not have any flaws, that never intimately knew sin, and will look at blinded eyes. This is why we must have the spirit of excellence in these last days. We have to put our homes in order. God isn't going to use a monkey or a dog to carry out His work and represent His name. He is going to use someone who is made in His image and His likeness.

Some of my church members think that I am fussing at them and putting them down. God has made it clear to me that it is time for us to get ourselves together because we are ambassadors of Christ. God is preparing to sweep and move in an awesome way. We must speak two languages. We must speak the native language of the citizens here, and we must have a Holy language, which is direct contact with our Savior. We must speak in tongues **(1Corinthians 2:1-16)**. We must change our minds to the mind that was in Jesus Christ. I'm sure that you don't believe that the devil is messing with you because you smell good and your hair is nice. The devil knows what is about to take place.

The history of the Bible tells us how God has always taken people who were less fortunate and didn't have any skills or qualifications to go forth in His name. If you recall **David (1 Samuel 17)** he didn't possess the skills to fight a giant. He didn't have excellent speaking skills, armor, or the mind of a soldier. He said that he came in the name that is above every name, the name that can stop bullets from penetrating through flesh, the name that would take Goliath down. David came in the name of the Lord.

SATAN'S WORK

If you have strayed from your calling, you've moved from the pulpit to the back door, and you need to understand that the body of Christ needs you. The Bible says that one can chase a thousand (TEXT?) Think about how many demons are in the world. One person is not going to chase all of these demons away. We need an army of men and women who will believe in God at any cost. If you have read it in the Word, you'd know that it is so. Therefore, do not allow anyone to stop you.

The devil is allowing spirits to creep upon people in order to distort and hold back the anointing that is within them because the devil knows that it is the anointing that destroys the yoke. To destroy means that there is no way to go back to get it; it has been wiped away. If someone is truly anointed, hands on you, and that issue will be destroyed. The devil is trying to capture the anointing. This is why I said that some of you had the devil coming after in three areas: the lust of the eye, the lust of the flesh, and the pride of life. He is attempting to distort the anointing that is within you. You don't even deserve the anointing, but it's there. It's there because when God gives you something, He doesn't take it back. The devil knows that if he can keep your mind off of God and on yourself when the lost souls come to you, they'll leave you in a worse condition. *Can you imagine going to a hospital to be healed and, hours later, you leave the same way?* You decide that next time, you'll try Tylenol or a home remedy. This is why people are staying home from church and watching TBN or simply praying.

I have a cousin who has been in so much confusion that he's decided that if he prays, he'll be all right. He said that the only difference between the people in the church and himself is that the people in the church aren't being real.

God is preparing to use the body of Christ in an awesome and profound way. Realize that it is not going to take a lot of people to start this fire. It doesn't take a lot of fire to burn down a building, and all it takes is the correct products. A small match can burn down a great building in a matter of minutes if you have the right stuff. Many of you have the right stuff, but you've been distracted. The devil has told you to go this way and that way. The reality is that there is only one way, and it's straight, and it's narrow. God wants to set you up and get you back on track. He wants you to know that He has made a way for you, and it's called grace. He said that His grace is sufficient. Today, what He wants you to do is come boldly to the throne of grace. Declare that you have no shame in what you have done and go to the throne boldly so that you may obtain mercy.

IT'S HARVEST TIME
John 4:31-38

Many times, when we really need the Lord, we go before Him, and we begin to beg. We ask the Lord to help us, increase our finances, give us a mate and a car, and help us survive. Take this question into mind. If someone was supposed to do something for you, and while staying faithful, you still blessed them, and you had been waiting for two thousand years for them to do what they said that they would do, and they still hadn't done it, would you at any time develop a bad attitude with that person? This situation is similar to that of parents and children. Parents feed and clothe their children, and their children are still not satisfied. Children are always begging their parents for something, and they know that the light, car note and mortgage bills have to be paid. Yet, they'll ask their parents for a pair of Nikes or a new hairdo.

Jesus is in the same situation. He has been waiting for almost two thousand years for something to happen. People slapped Him and spit on Him, and He left heaven to come to the earth, and the very thing that He had been waiting for, people were willing to help Him achieve.

People don't even pay attention to God, yet they go to Him on their knees asking for things like homes or a mate, even though they aren't ready for one. People ask God for a car, and they don't have money for gas, but they ask because they figure that God will provide the gas, too. God has been waiting for something to take place that He told His disciples would happen. It is now harvest time.

THE HARVEST IS RIPE, BUT THE LABORERS ARE FEW

If you know anything about farming, you know that you have to pick your crops at the right time, or you could lose them.

Luke 10:2 reads, "Therefore said he unto them, The harvest truly is great, but the laborers are few: pray ye, therefore, the Lord of the harvest, that he would send forth labourers into his harvest".

He knew that laborers didn't think the way that they wanted to think. A laborer is someone who will do whatever is asked of them. People who are given titles and positions think that they are too high and grand to perform the duties of a laborer. This is why Jesus wanted laborers instead of people with titles.

When Jesus began His ministry, he didn't stop at the homes of the priest and ask the priest to follow Him. He didn't stop at the Catholics' and Roman's homes because they already had titles and positions. Jesus needed laborers because His harvest was ripe, but His laborers were few.

If a farmer plants something, he wants everything that he reaps for himself. He watches his crops grow. He puts a scarecrow in the midst of his crops because he doesn't want birds to peck at them. He makes sure that he sprays pesticides on the fruit because he doesn't want pestilence to destroy them. Farmers have people watching over their crops so that no one else can destroy them.

We need to tell the Lord that we are ready to become laborers. If David had to wash the doors of the church, he wanted to be in God's presence. He knew that when God's presence came into the church, it would flow throughout the entire church. So, if he were inside the church, God would touch him too. However, there was a prophet and a preacher in the church. David knew that God wouldn't forget about him. I am reminded of **(Matthew 20)** when one laborer went forth to work twelve hours, and his master told him that he would be paid whatever was right. Another laborer arrived six hours later, and the master offered him the same pay. Someone may come to God hours after everyone else, knowing that they took their time getting there. Yet, they still ask God to save them, help them, make their heart clean, and renew in them a right spirit. God, knowing that they arrived during the last hour and loving them so much, He'll give them what everyone else received. Although Adam, Eve, John, and Paul were mistreated, God told them that in the last days, He would pay them the same wages.

We are the generation that God has been waiting for. God has waited for two thousand years. I'll be upset if I have to wait twenty-four hours. Jesus has been patiently waiting on us. Today, God is waiting for you. The only person that should control you is God. You have to be crazy to serve the devil. I know people get upset when I say that, but that is the way that I feel. Anyone who believes that they can be like God is stupid. *How can someone believe that they can be like God when God created them?* God knows every part of the devil, inside and out, and the devil believes that he can be like God. You have to be crazy to follow an idiot like that after I've shared with you that in my wrong, God kept my heart beating.

God wants you. The worst thing about it is that God will have you whether or not you come to Him. You are going to praise, worship, and serve Him. The decision is yours. You can do it in pleasure or torment.

> **Romans 14:11** reads, "For it is written, As I live, saith the Lord, every knee shall bow to me, and every tongue shall confess to God."

If you decide to go to hell, prepare to praise God in hell. Preachers don't preach about hell anymore. They're that people won't give a good offering. I don't care about the offering. I care about your soul.

The other day, I received a call; someone said that they had some money for me. At the time, I was out taking care of God's business, and as it's said, He'll take care of you when you give Him your heart, soul, and mind. He will reward you. When you go out to labor for Him, He will pay you, and when God adds to you, He adds no sorrow.

Do not allow this day to go by without giving your entire heart, soul, and mind to the Lord. If you need the Holy Ghost or maybe you've backslid, give your all to the Lord today. Preachers have things mixed up. Jesus ministered in preaching and teaching so that He could have a mass altar call. Jesus laid hands on people. He didn't tell the people to lift their hands and leap into the air three times and declare that they were coming out of their situation. If you want to be close to the Lord, surrender your life today. It's harvest time.

CONTROLLING YOUR SOUL

The word of the Lord speaks of a Samaritan woman who was at a well. I had always wondered why they would preach about the Samaritan woman, but I've finally received the revelation: Jesus was raised in racism. It is brought to my attention on national television that people are into racism. The word of the Lord declares that we are to love our enemies. Love is a state of action where you begin to make sacrifices, and Love is not spoken; it is shown.

When Jesus was raised, it was during a time when the Jews and the Samaritans didn't like one another. In the Bible, we find that Jesus was at the well with a Samaritan woman. The Samaritan woman asked Jesus why He was talking with her. He told her that there was a racial situation taking place that had been going on for generations and generations. He told her that she knew she wasn't supposed to be speaking to Him, but He couldn't live by the same standards that His forefathers lived by. He said that there was a harvest that needed to be picked right now. Some souls needed to be back in the hands of the Lord.

When you don't have control of your soul, you don't have control of your thoughts, mind, ways, or desires. This woman at the well was wondering why Jesus was talking to her. It was because her soul didn't love Jesus. He came for her that day, and she acted as if she didn't know what He was talking about. She told Jesus that He didn't know what He was talking about. Jesus told her that the five men that she had been with, including the one that she was with all the time, hadn't been able to satisfy her. She wasn't satisfied because she was searching for something that she couldn't find or have. She couldn't find it because it wasn't in a man, or a stroke of her hair, or a foot massage. She couldn't be satisfied because her soul was miserable and in trouble, Jesus had come for her soul. She was waiting for someone who was said to be the King of

Kings and the Lord of Lords. Jesus told her that she was speaking to that man.

This is why I tell young ladies that what they're looking for isn't in a man; and it's in God. Some women want a man to make them happy and satisfy them. I want you to know that a man cannot make you happy, nor can he satisfy you. If he doesn't possess his soul. Your soul consists of your feelings, mind, intellect, emotions, and thoughts. This woman at the well didn't have control of her emotions, and she was waiting for another lover. She was waiting for a man to come and save her soul. Unaware that she was talking to the lover of her soul, the man who loved her the most, and the man who cared about her enough to discuss the situation with her in public. Jesus didn't care about what His generation believed; He had to talk to the woman outside in the open. He loved her enough to surrender His throne, to give up the presence of heaven, and to come down to earth to save her soul.

Why was it that out of all of the fine men that she was with, none of them excited her the way that Jesus did? It was because they didn't have control over her soul. Jesus wasn't dealing with her soul. The woman had never felt that way before. She had six men to hold, touch, and kiss her, and none of them had ever made her feel the way that he made her feel. She decided to leave her water pots and tell everyone to come and meet a man who told her everything, that moved her, touched her, and held her, and His name is Jesus.

In these last and evil days, God is going to have vengeance on the devil because the souls that the devil has, he didn't do anything to deserve them. God came down from heaven and breathed life into those souls. The devil didn't do anything but persuade them to follow him.

Matthew 16:26a reads, "For what is a man profited, if he shall gain the whole world, and lose his own soul?"

Will you give a hug, a kiss, or money in exchange for your soul? Some of you have given your soul to the devil for a hug. You may ask how you did that; by hugging someone, you allowed them to enter into your most prized possession because they told you that you were cute or your hair was nice. You gave up the only thing that you had that was worth anything.

Matthew 16:26b reads, "…or what shall a man give in exchange for his soul?"

Now we're discussing profit. What would it profit you to gain a man who will squeeze you and hold you and, in exchange, lose your soul? It doesn't profit you anything because you're still not in control of your soul. Janet Jackson sang a song about being in control, but she really wasn't in control. She allowed people to affect her feelings, her emotions, and her heart.

It's time for us to regain control. How is it that someone can wink at you and cause you to give up your soul? How is it that someone can dance in front of you and cause you to give up your soul? How is it that a young lady can come before you with the right perfume and the right length of hair, and you'll give up your soul? Is it because you are not in control, and you aren't even aware of it? It's harvest time. This is the time that some of you are going to have your soul back. Everything that you are striving for, God will give it to you.

There is something that moves you when you are in control of your soul. People don't know why I'm so excited these days. It's because it's strictly God and I. It's not God and I and she and her and it; no one else has control of my soul. No one else is going to make me upset or reach into my soul any longer.

Too many of us allow people to reach into our souls too easily. How is it that someone can reach into your soul so easily? If someone doesn't shake your hand when you see them, they'll be inside your soul, emotions, and feelings. People open up their souls and allow others to walk into them.

That is how the devil has been controlling us. We don't have enough information about our souls. The soul is your only prize possession. The Bible tells us to hide the word in your heart. Some of you know that your heart is beating, but you never seen it because it's hidden under your flesh. It's your body's most prized possession. Your heart pumps blood throughout your body. Why do you think that God said for us to hide His word in our hearts? It's because He wants it to be able to flow throughout your body the way that your blood does.

We have to get our souls back at any cost. The reason why we are not prospering is because someone else has our soul. When a young man winks his eye, we go to him. When a young woman calls, we go to her. Someone else has control of our emotions and our feelings.

You don't know why you're still in that broke and raggedy car, still allowing money to control you or still allowing them to control you.

3 John 1:2 reads, "Beloved, I wish above all things that thou mayest prosper and be in health, even as thy soul prospereth."

"Beloved" means I still love you regardless of "Even as," which means that it has to come around. The problem is that our souls are not prospering. Some of our souls are in trouble or headed to hell. It's time that our souls prosper.

When you are in control of your soul, you are in the hands of and the presence of God. The devil doesn't want you to have control over your soul. He wants your emotions and your feelings to run out of the door. He'd rather you have control of your shout, your ability to speak in tongues, or your ability to wave your hands. The devil knows that the day that we gain control over our souls and our minds, he'll be out of business. You know that you can walk away from the devil, and you don't have to look his way or talk to him because you have control over your soul. When you have control over your soul, you can make your flesh, thoughts, and heart obey you.

Philippians 2:5 reads, "Let this mind be in you, which was also in Christ Jesus:"

When you gain control of your mind, you will able to proclaim that you can do all things through Christ who strengthens you.

(Philippians 4:13).

When you are serving the Lord, and you're in control of your soul, if you seek Him first and His righteousness, He will add everything to you. The devil is on the same level that we are on. The

The devil has to report to God and receive permission and instructions from God in the same way that we have to. So, why are we listening to someone who is in the same position that we're in? If a poor man came into your church and tried to tell you how to become rich quickly, you wouldn't listen to him. The devil has no home, heaven, or hell.

God is in control of hell, heaven, and everything else. We need to tell the devil that enough is enough. When we gain control of our souls, God will give us prosperity. God hasn't forgotten about you. Joy is coming.

Psalms 30:5 reads, "For his anger endureth but a moment; in his favour is life; weeping may endure for a night, but joy cometh in the morning.

Since I've had my soul back, I've risen to another level. Sex and television are no longer controlling me. I have my soul back. I can declare that my soul loves Jesus. For in the name of Jesus, dead men are going to rise, finances are going to change, healing and miracles are going to come.

REPRODUCTION
Matthew 7:15-23

The word of the Lord declares that a good tree can not bring forth evil fruit. The Bible tells us how we are to live our lives and what type of examples we should give to others. Many people claim that they are Christians. To be a Christian means to be Christ-like.

Today, churches are not producing Christ-like people. Churches are reproducing backbiters, liars, and fornicators. If we were doing what we were supposed to be doing reproductively, we would walk into hospitals, and patients would walk out with us. There would be no convalescent homes. We would conquer communities that gangs had taken over. The problem is that we don't truly believe what the word of the Lord says. The Bible says that a good tree can not bring forth evil fruit. Therefore, people who claim that they are Christians should only bear good fruit. Every act that Jesus did was a good act. I have read of Him going to a city and turning it upside down. Thousands of people would gather around Him because they wanted what He had to offer. Jesus offered them power, anointing, joy, peace, and kindness. If we are to be Christ-like, we, too, must possess all of those things. We can not mix good with evil. If you claim that you are being Christ-like, people need to see the same things that followed Christ following you.

Philippians 2:5 reads, "Let this mind be in you, which was also in Christ Jesus:"

Something has happened in our churches that has changed our minds from the mind Christ possessed. His mind was focused on gaining all of the lost souls at any cost. He knew that there were too many blind, sick, and deaf people.

There came a point in Jesus's life when His father, Joseph, died, and he took over his father's carpenter's business. During the time of Jesus' childhood, a son did the same work that his father did. The twist in Jesus' situation is that he had to be about His Father's business. Not His Father, Joseph, but His Father in heaven **(John 5:36)**. When Jesus gathered twelve men and began to do the work of His Father. His mother came to Him and asked Him to return home with her.

Matthew 12:50 reads, "For whosoever shall do the will of my Father which is in heaven, the same is my brother and sister. And mother."

Jesus told His brother that the work that He was doing was what His father wanted Him to do. He was supposed to find and save the lost souls, heal the sick, and open blind eyes.

Many people will try to mislead us concerning the work that we are to do as Christians. We are not supposed to criticize, whine, fuss, and complain. There is too much work for us to do. We have to have the mind that Jesus had. Jesus never ceased to contemplate what He had been sent to earth to do. There are so many preachers now who claim that they need a break or a vacation. The only time that I have read where Jesus had what we refer to as a break is when He went into the mountains to pray and seek His Father. He didn't go into the mountains to kick His feet up. When Jesus prayed, He was so far into the spirit that He knew exactly what was happening with His disciples. Jesus was in tune with what was taking place around Him. If we were in tune with the things that are taking place around us, our minds wouldn't be off track. We wouldn't be worried about who was doing what. The only thing that we would be concerned with doing would be our jobs.

In the church, when someone creates a program, and no one joins them in bringing it to pass, they develop an attitude. Jesus went to His Father in prayer and asked Him to take away the bitter cup that He was holding **(Luke 22:42)**. Jesus had all of the words of sin inside of one cup, and He had to drink it. At the end of His journey, the three men who had followed Him couldn't even stay awake long enough to pray with Him. Those three disciples had heard the voice of God and seen His manifestation. Wouldn't you think that Jesus would have an attitude? He didn't develop an attitude because He knew that He had a job to do.

You have to understand that when you have a job to do, you can not be concerned with what other people are doing. You have to remain focused on what you have to do. Paul was in jail, but he continued to write letters to the churches. Paul had been mistreated, and the men who were supposed to be with Him had abandoned Him, yet he still fought a good fight. Paul finished his course and kept his faith. Sometimes, you have to keep your faith regardless of what is taking place around you, who's talking about you, or who's putting you down.

We, who are Christians, are the only light that the world knows. We are the light of the world. Regardless of who follows us or who doesn't, our light will continue to shine bright. Simply because people don't join up with you doesn't mean that you don't possess a light that men can be drawn to. Tell them that if they join you, both of you have the ability to create a brighter light and carry it into the greater amount of darkness. A car with two lights is better than a car with one light. On the same note, a car that has only one light is still able to arrive at its destination with one brightly shining light.

Those of us who are living in the Christian world are going to have to change. When people follow you, what do you think they are receiving from you? What type of feedback or response do your followers receive from you? We need to change to the point that men and women will want to be like us. Consider this: If people were to follow you every day, *what type of people would they be? How would they talk? What type of faith would they have? What type of things would they see? What would they hear you talk about when you were on the same telephone? What things would they hear in your car or bedroom?*

Everywhere Jesus went, He was a perfect example. When His disciples found Him at the well with the Samarian woman, He was ministering. The woman didn't leave him and tell the people that he did some perverse thing with her. She told the people to come and hear a man that had told her everything about herself **(John 4)**.

Jesus knew what His mission in life was. Sometimes, we forget what our mission and our purpose is. We may come to church, and someone may have an attitude, and when you ask them what is bothering them, you find yourself listening to a lot of sad stories. When the conversation is over, you end up feeling the same way they felt.

Your mind frame has to be correct. You can be around the best and not be the best. The disciples were around the best, yet they couldn't do what they saw Jesus do **(Matthew 17:14-21)**. Jesus told them that some things came by prayer and fasting. Since the disciples had the best of them, they didn't make any sacrifices. When it comes to prayer and fasting, everyone is not going to join you. The disciples had Jesus with them and still had a problem fasting and praying. Therefore, if men had a problem praying and fasting with Jesus, I'm sure they would have a problem without Him. Some people are striving to achieve perfection, so there is no need to develop an attitude when no one wants to pray and fast with you. There are some things that you will have to do alone.

The question is, do you believe? A believer will stand on absolutely nothing. Peter had to believe in Jesus to step out of his boat onto the water **(Mark 4:35-41)**. Shadrach, Meshach, and Abednego had to believe in God to say that even if God didn't do what they asked Him to do, they knew the God had the ability to do it **(Daniel 3:17-18)**. By walking with God, we are declaring that we believe in

Him. There are people and churches that you can not follow because they don't truly believe in God. There once was a day in time that before someone would go to the hospital, they would have a man of God pray for them. These days, people will be in the hospital for two weeks and will never call their pastor because they're in the care of a doctor.

If you don't truly believe in what you are doing for God, you should stop today. Don't waste your time playing games in church. Your desire should be to become a reproducer. When people are around you, reproduce righteousness, holiness, belief, signs, and wonders in them. You will have to change. We all will have to change. As I began to study this text, I told the Lord that I had to change. I don't want my son to grow up and beat women because he watched me do it. Then, he'll tell people that he's like his father. I affect people regardless of whether it's in a good way or an evil way. You should do the same thing.

Some of us stand in the way of sinners. A sinner may want to live right, but they are constantly seeing you backslide. A young man once said, "I don't want they [have]. They're playing church. They're in and out every week. [That] makes me think [that] God [isn't] real."

What are you going to be able to say when you are bowing before Jesus, and God tells you that you stood in the way of your neighbor because you wouldn't, right? Or that you reproduced someone who was wavering and didn't believe in Him. God wants men and women who believe in Him and will stand on His word. That is why He makes a way out of no way. That is why we had Daniels and Moses'. Moses stood on God's word.

What are you reproducing? How are your children being raised? That question began to bother me. I do not want my children to witness me living a fake lifestyle. I don't want them to speak in tongues one minute and dance at the club the next minute because they've watched me do it. We'll all end up in hell. I want them to know that their father lives a holy and righteous life. Please don't take that statement as if I'm patting myself on the back. I am striving to achieve perfection. I'm working out my soul salvation with fear and trembling. If I come short of the glory of God, I am brave enough to admit it and ask for forgiveness. If I have to repent every day, I'll do that because, throughout the day, people are watching me and following me. Someone may need a way out, and I may be able to help them find it; therefore, I can not stand in their way.

I was fasting one day, and I began to crave a box of hot tamale candy. Sister Jana Smith of my church said, "Pastor, you can't have candy."

"Look, I've been on this fast long enough.", I said.

"No, you can't do that, pastor. You've told people that you're fasting because the Lord has told you to."

Simple things that you do can affect and throw others off track.

If you testify one Sunday and someone hears your testimony, they know that if God blessed you, God will have to bless them, too.

Hebrews 10:25 reads, "Not forsaking the assembling of ourselves together, as the manner of some *is*; but exhorting *one another*: and so much more, as ye see the day approaching,"

Two are better than one. What you do can encourage someone else to go on a little further. We affect one another; hence, we need to stop playing games in church.

Throughout our walk with God, we have to purge ourselves. Too many times, we depend on other people to help us and draw us to God. Sometimes, we have to go to Jesus on our own and tell him that we need Him to help us, make a way out for us, and change us. Too often, when we're around one another, we don't present who we truly are. Peter didn't reveal who he actually was when he was around Jesus. He always acted as if he was big and bad. He told Jesus that he would stand up for Him. When it became time to put the rubber to the road, we found out that Peter was an exceptional coward and good at running away and hiding **(Matthew 26:57-75)**. Peter couldn't do what he said that he would do because he tried to show off in front of his peers. Peter was the disciple who was the greatest among them **(Matthew 18:1-9)**. Peter always wanted to be at the forefront and be great and mighty.

The question here is, *what will happen when tests and trials come and there is no one around you? Will you still stand for Jesus?* It's time for us to stop trying to impress man and begin to do things for Jesus. I've decided to live my life for Jesus. Sometimes, I'm tired, and I don't come to church with my mind made up to worship God.

Sometimes, I don't want to go to church, but when I enter the house of the Lord, my mind begins to change, and something begins to grow inside of me. I become like Jeremiah. I want to throw in the towel, but the word of the Lord comes to me again in a strong way.

> **Psalms 23:6** reads. "Surely goodness and mercy shall follow me all the days of my life: and I will dwell in the house of the Lord for ever."

I hear God say that he will bless me and make way for me. When I'm down and out, God reminds me that greater is He that is in me, that He that is of the world **(1 John 4:4)**. Sometimes, God has to talk to me and remind me that I am more than a conqueror. When I'm weak and feeling down, God tells me to say that I am strong and he'll give me strength.

There is no need for me to try to convince you that this walk with God is easy. This is the most important walk that a man can take.

It's hard, straight, and narrow. During this day and hour, you have to live life one day at a time and stop trying to live by weeks and months.

Each day is a day that the Lord has made, and you need to rejoice and be glad on that day. You have to live holy today. You can't be concerned with tomorrow when it's a struggle to make it through today. You have to be an example today.

What type of fruit have you been producing? Is the fruit on your tree good, or is it rotten and nasty? I have a cousin who once said,

"[My] fruit is poisoned. I'm in the shape that I'm in because I poisoned a lot of people. I listen to you [preach] every day on the radio, but I poison [people]."

What has grown from you? Is it negativity? Who has followed you into your church lately? The Lord wants us to go into the world and make disciples. The number one job in the world is to convert sinners into saints, and that job is yours. Today, whatever it takes for you to be back on track, you need to do. Jesus is soon to return **(Luke 21:27).**

IF EVERYONE WON ONE, THEN EVERYONE WOULD BE WON

Acts 2:47
Ezekial 18:4

INTRODUCTION

Acts 2:47 reads, "Praising God, and having favour with all the people. And the Lord added to the church daily such as should be saved."

Ezekial 18:4 reads, "Behold, all souls are mine: as the soul of the father, so also the soul of the son is mine: the soul that sinneth, it shall die."

We must first understand what God is saying to us in the book of Ezekial before we understand what He is saying to us in the book of Acts. God begins Ezekial 18:4 by saying, "Behold . . ."

To behold means to apprehend by the use of the eyes. To apprehend something that you see means to understand what you are looking at. The word behold means that when you look upon something, you understand what you are looking at.

God that goes further to say, " . . all souls are mine:"

God wants us to look out into the harvest at the people with pink and green hair and the people with body piercings and tattoos. He wants us to look at the things that are going on with the people and understand that every one of their souls belongs to Him. The soul of the prostitute, the homosexual, and even the child molester belongs to Him. When you really understand this concept, you will see that the only thing that sustains you is the blood that has been placed on you.

What is being described in **Acts 2:47** is during a time when the people were praising God and having favour with all of the people because God had released the Holy Ghost. (TEXT?) reads, after the holy ghost comes upon you, you shall receive power."

You will have the power to go back and bring the people that you hung out with to God. You have the power to go back into the world and find the girl you had sex with, the boys you drank with, and the people you fornicated with and bring them back to God. This is why I've titled this chapter **<u>If Everyone Won One, then Everyone Would Be Won.</u>"**

God didn't give you the Holy Ghost only to fight your problems because this fight goes beyond your problems. He gave you the Holy Ghost so that you may be a witness unto Him (TEXT?)."

If everyone that God converts would win one soul, and that person wins a soul and that person wins a soul, then every soul would be won.

SATAN'S WORK

Anything that God does in the beginning, He is going to do in the end. God had a personal relationship with Adam in the Garden of Eden. In the cool of the evening, God would come down and fellowship with Adam. The devil became upset when he witnessed the relationship that Adam had with God. The devil wanted to end that relationship because he wanted to be like God and exalt his throne above God's throne. The devil was intelligent enough to know not to try to end the relationship by using Adam, so he used Eve. The devil decided that he would have the same relationship that God had with Adam, with Eve. The devil approached Eve in the form of a snake. The snake was familiar to Eve, and she wasn't afraid of the snake. She had become comfortable with conversing with a snake. The devil decided that he would draw her away from God. This is how the devil has been since God began a relationship with man. The devil wants to draw us away from God so that he can have a relationship with us.

God did not send Jesus down here so that today we can fellowship with the devil or for us to have our problems taken care of.

God sent Jesus to earth because he wanted all of the souls to have a relationship with Him.

The devil begins to toy with us, and we begin to think in the same manner as Eve did. We look at our surroundings and complain about those things that we don't have. We talk back to the devil when he speaks to us. By doing this, we can't go into the world and save souls because we are focusing on ourselves. The devil begins to remind us that we don't have a car, we don't have enough clothing, and our hair isn't long enough, and we listen to him. Many of us fall right into the devil's traps because we don't know who we are in Christ.

SOUL WINNING

God decided long ago that He was going to have a personal relationship with all souls regardless of whether or not men choose to accept Him.

The situation that we are in is one in which God has a relationship with us, but He wants us to have a relationship with Him. God recognizes that human beings can only develop a relationship with Him when they have experienced struggles, pain, and salvation and are sent into the world with testimony.

Your testimony is not for your church to hear. Instead, it is what the Lord has done for you and for the people in the world to hear. The people who are in the church are saved and being blessed by God the same way that you are. Testimonies are for those people who have yet to have a personal experience where God has done something special in their lives. You are to take your testimony into the world and tell them of God's goodness and what He's done for you.

IT'S IN YOUR PRAISE

Acts 2:47 begins by saying, "Praising God . . ."

There is something unique about when you begin to praise God. Anyone who praises God is remembering what God has done for them. Anytime that you begin to praise God, you remember where the Lord has brought you from. The problem is that we are not praising God enough. We have started to allow the devil to come into our lives, fool us, and throw us off track. If your mind is constantly on the Lord, you won't slip and fall, and you won't be pulled off track.

Can you imagine how Peter felt to realize he had the same power as Jesus? The same power that Jesus used to heal the soldier's ear when Peter had cut it off, Peter now had. The devil doesn't want us to know how powerful we are. He doesn't want us to know that we are supposed to go back out into the world and win souls. We are not supposed to worry about our problems.

When Paul realized what God was using him for, he concluded that it was O.K. if he was in prison and that his brethren didn't visit him. Paul decided that while he was in prison, he would write letters and encourage people and give God all that he could give Him.

In this day and time, the church needs to give God all that we can give Him. We have to be excited about what God is doing. These people in the book of Acts were praising God because they were excited about what Jesus had done. They were excited that Jesus had suffered and gone through pain and ridicule, and now what was in Christ was in them.

When you praise God, you bring Him into your atmosphere. If a bill that you couldn't pay were to come to your house, do you believe that God would love to see you begin to praise Him because you know He's going to pay for it? You knew that by receiving the bill, you just gave God an opportunity to come through for you.

All of the great men who were there when the Holy Ghost came knew that it was another opportunity for God to do something. This is why they began to praise God. They knew that they had obstacles and men who didn't like them, yet they still had praise inside of them. It was an opportunity for God to take a negative situation and make it a positive situation.

Anytime that you give God praise, regardless of the situation, favour will follow you. Our text tells us that the people have been having lately. Maybe your praise has been hindered lately.

THE CHURCH

What happens when you have praise and favour in your church? God begins to add people to the church. At this point in time, God can not add people to the church the way he wants to. God is the one who touches the hearts of men. The reason that God can not add to the church daily is that there is not enough praise in the church, nor is there any favour following us. God can not attach souls to us until we change and realize that life isn't about us.

If Paul had been concerned with what he was going through, we would not have many of the scriptures in the New Testament, or God would have used someone else. Even while Paul was afflicted, he wrote to us and told us how to stay saved. God doesn't want us to dwell on our problems because there are souls in the world who are attached to us. We need to praise God and have favour so that He can add those souls to the body of Christ. God can not bring His most prized possession into the church where people won't pray, fast, worship, or give Him the praise.

God wants us to realize that we who are in the church know the entire truth and what we need to do in order to succeed. There are organizations in this world who only know half of the truth, but no one can change the half that they do have. God can not bring his souls into the church because the church will taint and contaminate them with bad spirits. This is why the Apostolic movement in this day and age is a disgrace to when it first began. God is sending his souls to the people who only have half of the truth because when His souls walk into the church, the people in the church smile; before the service begins, they are praying to God out of obedience; they are in church constantly.

This started when Jesus walked on this earth. Jesus didn't go to the temple and ask the pastor or those who were praying to walk with Him. Jesus went and found sinners to walk with Him because he knew that they would be crazy enough to go into the world and bring back all of the souls that they could. He didn't want people who would look at someone's green hair or that they were a lesbian or they drank too much and not want to win their soul. God doesn't want a lot of stiff-necked, hard-hearted people. God wants people who realize that it was only by the grace of God that they were saved.

> **Luke 22:31** reads, "And the Lord said, Simon, Simon, behold, Satan hath desired to have you, that he may sift you as wheat: But I have prayed fro thee, that thy faith fail not: and when thou art converted, strengthen thy brethren."

Here, we read that Jesus told Simon that Satan wanted to have him. To have someone means to have an intimate relationship with them. Satan wanted to have Simon so caught up that Simon didn't know what the devil was preparing to do to him. Jesus told Simon that He had already prayed for him. In the church, we have people who talk too much. Everything that they see is not to be told. Jesus simply told Peter that He had prayed for him. Jesus, under the anointing, didn't criticize Peter. Why do we criticize one another? Why don't we pray?

These days, we don't believe that sinners are supposed to come into the church and be converted. We must go back to Acts 2:47, which tells us that the Lord added to the church daily such things that *should* be saved. Jesus knew that Peter wasn't saved. This is why Jesus told him that *after* he is converted, he should strengthen his brethren. His brethren were sinners. Jesus wanted Peter to go back and save the people he used to hang around because all the self-righteous people weren't going to save them.

> Jesus said, "But I have prayed for thee, that thy faith fail not:"

> **Matthew 17:20** reads, "And Jesus said unto them, Because of your unbelief: for verify I say unto you, if ye have faith as a grain of mustard seed, ye shall say unto this mountain, Remove hence to yonder place; and it shall remove; and nothing shall be impossible unto you."

(TEXT?) Without faith, it is impossible to please God.

Although Peter wasn't saved, he still managed to grab onto a little faith. After Jesus had been crucified, Peter backslid and began fishing again. Mary came down to Peter's boat, and through Mary,

Peter was able to hear the voice of God, and he began to search for Jesus. Anytime that you begin to search for Jesus, you will find Him.

Matthew 7:7, "Ask, and it shall be given you: seek, and ye shall find; knock, and it shall be opened unto you:"

These days, there is such a fuss concerning women ministers.

Mary searched for Jesus when she didn't find Him in the tomb.

Consider this. At the time of the resurrection, Mary became the first woman to preach a message. Her message wasn't long. Mary expressed that men had run and attempted to hide from Jesus. Mary told the men that she looked for Jesus and she had a message from heaven. She told the people that Jesus had risen and that they needed to come back with her and see him.

When Peter heard the things that Mary said, Peter knew that it had to be Jesus speaking through her. Peter knew that although he wasn't saved, he had to return with Mary.

> **Matthew 11:28-30** reads, "Come unto me, all ye that labor and are heavy laden, and I will give you rest. Take my yoke upon you, and learn of me; for I am meek and lowly in heart: and ye shall find rest unto your souls. For my yoke is easy, and my burden is light."

In the church, we make things difficult by placing too many demands on people. We want God to change them instantly. The people in the church want men and women to be saved, sanctified, holy, and magnifying God, but we don't do the same things. Jesus was a living example for us. It is time for us to stop playing church.

(TEXT? Reads do not add or take away."

I feel sorry for men, women, bishops, and pastors who have added to and taken away from the word of the Lord. God is the one who adds souls to the church. Through studying this text, I received revelation. I made the mistake of adding to God's Word. I was told that no one could become a member of my church unless they had been baptized and filled with the Holy Ghost. People came to join the church, and we turned them away because they hadn't been saved or delivered. We have been taught wrong. God said that He added to the church daily, such as <u>SHOULD</u> be saved. These people should be saved, not turned away.

Sometimes, men and women have to be like Paul and die daily so that they can be saved. Some people have been in church for forty years and are just now being saved. They had been in church but still living in sin, and God turned them around after forty years so that they finally can go to heaven.

We can't worry about what others are doing and what they are saying. We can't look down on other people because they aren't saved.

Who are we to look down on someone else? Turn around and glance back down the hallway of your life and see where you came from.

This is why Peter could win souls. Peter remembered that in spite of all of his wrongs, Jesus still loved him. Jesus still put the gift into the world and won souls.

In this day and time, we are going to have to go into the world and begin to save souls. The church has become too selfish and self-centered. We care too much about ourselves, our problems, and what we are going through. When are we going to realize that Jesus has already paid the price and sacrificed so that we can go into the world and win souls and not be overwhelmed with our problems? It is time for the body of Christ to stop worrying about our cares, feelings, and worries.

(TEXT?) The flesh and spirit war against each other."

If God knows that there is a constant battle taking place within us, who are we to put someone down? Every time we find ourselves doing wrong, the first thing that we ask Jesus to do is to forgive us. We ask him not to hold our wrongs against us. Someone came into my office one day and told me that I needed to sit down in the midst of a war.

When we are sitting, there is no way for the Holy Spirit to be stirred up inside of you.

FROM THE PAST INTO THE FUTURE

The only way that we can go out and win souls is for us to win ourselves. We've gone far too off track. Some of us need to give ourselves back to God so that we can do our work.

As I studied this, God began to speak to me concerning my church. God said, "[There is] a spirit that [is] in this ministry, [and people] won't even forgive themselves."

People dwell on their past for too long. I caught myself doing it one morning. I found myself going to God about something that I had already told Him that I was sorry for.

When you are disobedient to God, the devil will tell you that your disobedience is the reason why you are not being blessed. As I was about to pray, God said, "What are you talking about?" I [have forgiven] you once. How many times do you want me to tell you? I don't even know what you [are] talking about. What are you talking about?"

I began to laugh at myself. Why would I go to God concerning something that He had already forgiven me for? How many times have we gone to God concerning the same things? We forget that God no longer remembers what He has forgiven us for. We can not go into the world to win souls, focusing on how the devil tricked us two years ago.

It is amazing how quickly Paul realized these things. Why does God use sinners to do an awesome and mighty work? It's because sinners believe in God. If God says that He has forgiven them, they believe it. People who are in church sit in the church so long that they forget who God really is. It only took Paul three days to become converted, and they began preaching.

You have to have faith that God can and will use you. By God holding on to Peter, the world began to turn back to God. God wants someone who will ask God to use them despite their sins. Someone who desires to be anointed and touched by God. (TEXT?) upon this rock, and the gates of hell shall not prevail against it."

Your lifestyle may not be close to Peter's lifestyle, and God wants to know if you will allow Him to use you. Will you allow Him to take you into the streets and have you compel men to come to God? Will you allow him to take you into the street and bring you up your past because your past will block his ability to use you? Will you allow your past to be used to draw people to God?

There is something about going through something and being converted and recognizing someone who is going through the same thing that you went through. This is going through the same thing that you went through. This is what happened to Simon (Peter) when God told him to go out and strengthen his brethren after he was converted. Simon knew what his brethren were going through. Simply looking at what you went through as a sinner and the misery that you experienced should make you want to go out and win souls. Some men and women were abused and misused and tried to take their lives to escape their situation. You know how it feels to be a backslider and come to church and have people look down on you, not want to shake your hand and talk about you.

I will never forget the time that I went to church, and no one shook my hand. True enough, I was full of the devil, but I wanted help.

No one came and asked me how I was doing. I felt like I had a disease.

The pastor didn't even shake my hand.

We should want to win souls once we are converted. We are the lights of this world that sit upon a hill and can not be hidden.

How many sinners do we pass on the way to church?

Sometimes, we become too complacent and relaxed in the house of the Lord, and we forget where we came from. We say that we love the Lord, but we won't go into the world and win the souls of the sinners. We come to church and lay hands on the same person for 15 years, and they still haven't changed, but when a sinner comes in off of the street, we don't have time for them.

The Lord said to me, "You're wasting time on [people] that don't want to change, and the ones that want to change, you don't even want to deal with them because the devil has you sidetracked [and] looking [at people] who want to [act] up. You're worried about them."

I heard a man say, "For every twelve [church] members, there is a Judas. So just be ready. You have eleven good ones and one devil, and [he] comes to make you strong [and] to help you."

Have you ever noticed how easily we can put people down? It's because we are not going through what they are going through. It's because the devil has left our lives for a season. We forget that he'll be back, and he'll return more potent than before. You can not speak badly concerning other people because the devil will come and try you. While the devil has left you for a season, go out and try to bring everyone back into the fold. When the devil is in your life, it is during that time that you hold on to God's unchanging hand.

Consider this. When the devil was tempting Jesus, he wasn't out-calling meetings. Jesus followed the devil when he was struggling with temptation and looked at what the devil offered Him. Jesus was tempted from all points. To be drawn means to have a desire to do something or to want to do something that you shouldn't do. People feel guilty because the devil is tempting them, and they shouldn't because Jesus was tempted, too.

If everyone won one, then everyone would be defeated. In this day and time, people need God to be in their lives. We need to go into the world and win souls. None of us are perfect, yet God has called us to become a part of a worldwide calling.